AF235324

THE AMERICAN DREAM

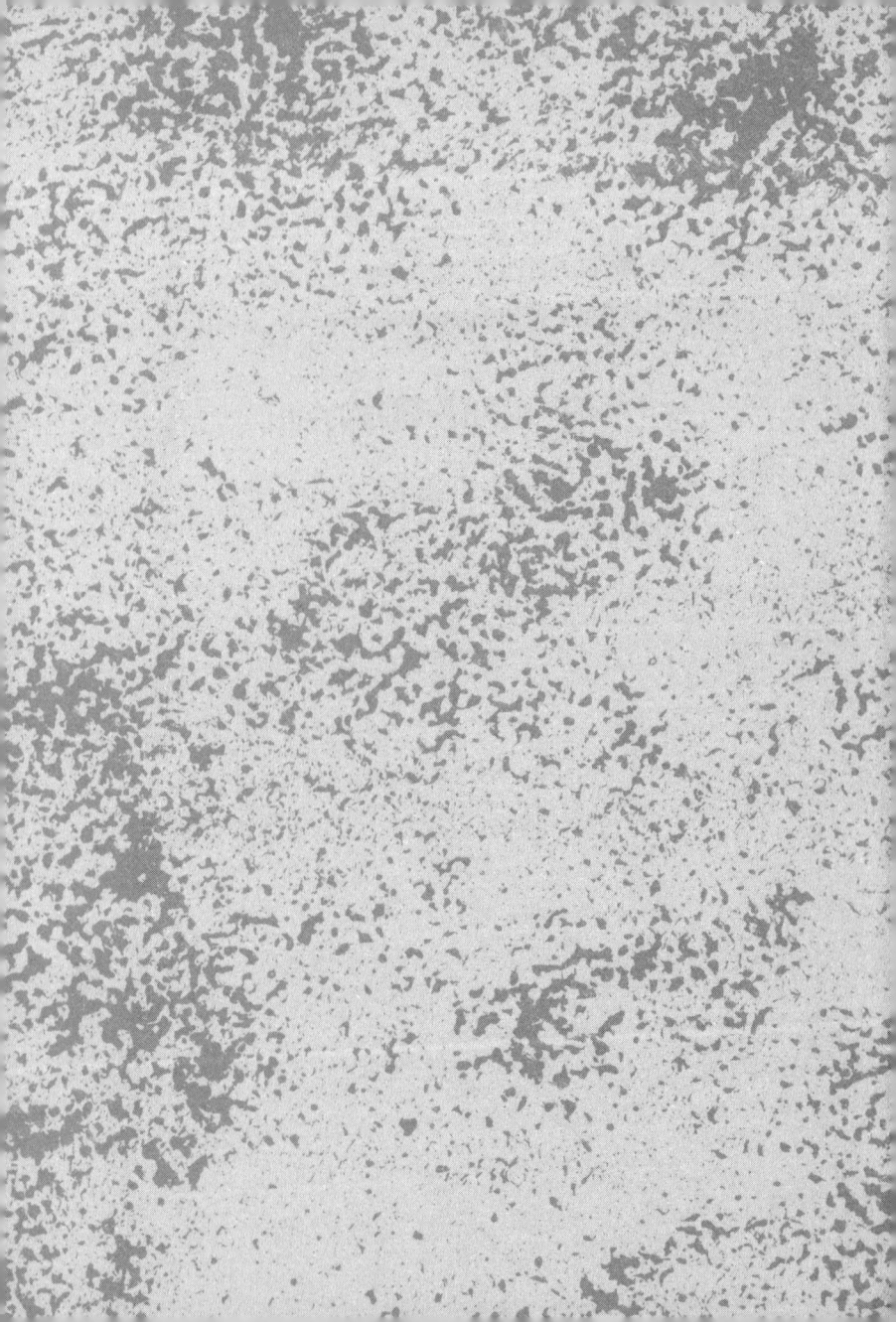

DR. MARTIN LUTHER KING JR.

THE AMERICAN DREAM

MartinLuther King Jr. *Library*

MartinLuther
KingJr.*Library*

In Association With **IPM**
INTELLECTUAL PROPERTIES
MANAGEMENT, INC.

License granted by Intellectual Properties Management, Inc., Atlanta, GA, exclusive licensor of The King Estate.

HarperCollins books may be purchased for educational, business, or sales promotional use. For information, please email the Special Markets Department at SPsales@harpercollins.com.

hc.com

Designed by Jason Kayser
Art © Rawpixel.com/stock.adobe.com

Library of Congress Cataloging-in-Publication Data has been applied for.

ISBN 978-0-06-346902-0

Printed in the United States of America

26 27 28 29 30 LBC 5 4 3 2 1

Foreword

By Yolanda Renee King

When my grandfather Martin Luther King Jr. delivered his commencement speech "The American Dream" at Lincoln University on June 6, 1961, President John F. Kennedy had been in office less than six months.

It was a hopeful time for much of America. And despite the continuing violence of racial segregation, Kennedy had become a symbol of progressive change. My grandfather began his speech to the Lincoln University graduates with an affirmation: "America is essentially a dream, a dream yet unfulfilled. It is a dream of a land where men of all races, of all nationalities and all creeds can live together as brothers." Of course, in those days, his reference to "men" meant all of humanity, including women and children.

Two years before his "I Have a Dream" speech at the Lincoln Memorial, my grandfather repeatedly cited "the American dream" in the commencement speech. He saw it as an unmet challenge for our nation to live up to its noblest ideals and principles, as stated in the Declaration of Independence: "We hold these truths to be self-evident, that all men are created equal, that they are endowed by their Creator with certain unalienable Rights, that among these are Life, Liberty and the pursuit of Happiness." My grandfather added, "This is the dream."

He noted, however, that "On the one hand we have proudly professed the principles of democracy, and on the other hand we have sadly practiced the very antithesis of those principles." He asserted his deeply held belief that "if America is to remain a first-class nation she can no longer have second-class citizens. . . . But now more than ever before, America is challenged to bring this noble dream into reality. . . . And so those who are working to implement the American dream are the true saviors of democracy." These words echo across the decades that have passed since then with prophetic relevance to our present day.

In our times, it is critically important that we never let go of this precious dream, because we can't have a functioning country without it. Every great nation needs a unifying principle, a set of core beliefs and a vision to rally all citizens around. We have in recent times, as well as in the past, experienced efforts to destroy this dream to benefit those who profit from dividing Americans along racial lines.

In the speech, my grandfather goes into detail to spell out the impressive achievements of African Americans, despite the brutal history of slavery, segregation and oppression. He calls on all Americans to recognize the common humanity of all people, regardless of their race or religion.

He chronicled the remarkable accomplishments of the nonviolent civil rights movement. "In less than a year, more than 142 cities of the Deep South have integrated their lunch counters, and this was done without a single court suit. It was done without spending millions and millions of dollars." He noted the success of the campaigns to desegregate public transportation and the result: "The attorney general of this nation has called on ICC to issue new regulations making it positively clear that segregation in interstate travel is illegal and unconstitutional."

My grandfather addressed the need for both education and legislation to eradicate the scourge of racism in our society. "Even though morality may not be legislated," he said, "behavior can be regulated. . . . We need religion and education to change attitudes and to change the hearts of men. We need legislation and federal action to control behavior. It may be true that the law can't make a man love me, but it can keep him from lynching me, and I think that's pretty important also." •

But we must remain ever vigilant in nonviolent

opposition to all forms of racial injustice. I emphasize nonviolence because it is the only method for resisting evil that is commensurate with our best ideals of brotherhood and sisterhood. Indeed, nonviolence is the only strategy that can make the dream a reality in America.

"If we seek to break down the system, we must do it with the proper methods," my grandfather said to the graduates. "I am convinced more than ever before that, as the powerful, creative way opens, men and women who are willing to break the barriers of oppression and of segregation and discrimination, they need not fall down to the levels of violence. They need not sink into the quicksands of hatred. They can stand on the high ground of noninjury, love and soul force, and turn this nation upside down and right side up."

As my father, Martin Luther King III, has recently said, "All of the victories of the civil rights movement were achieved with a no-nonsense commitment to nonviolence on the part of the demonstrators. . . . We must remember that even one act of violence will be used to justify expanding repression. We must always exercise nonviolent discipline in protesting against injustice. This requires that we make sure that all demonstrators get training in nonviolence and that they understand that nonviolence is the key to successful protest, and really, the preservation of our precious democracy."

Our country must forever be the beacon of hope that lights the way forward to a better future for all people. Above all, let us keep faith that God is with us in this nonviolent movement.

Faith, courage and love for all people. As we go

forward into the uncertain future, let us hold close these values that will sustain us in our struggle against tyranny, in our movement for love, justice and freedom in the spirit of Martin Luther King Jr. and in our sacred quest to make the American dream a reality for all.

"THE AMERICAN DREAM"
SPEECH

June 6, 1961
Lincoln University
Pennsylvania

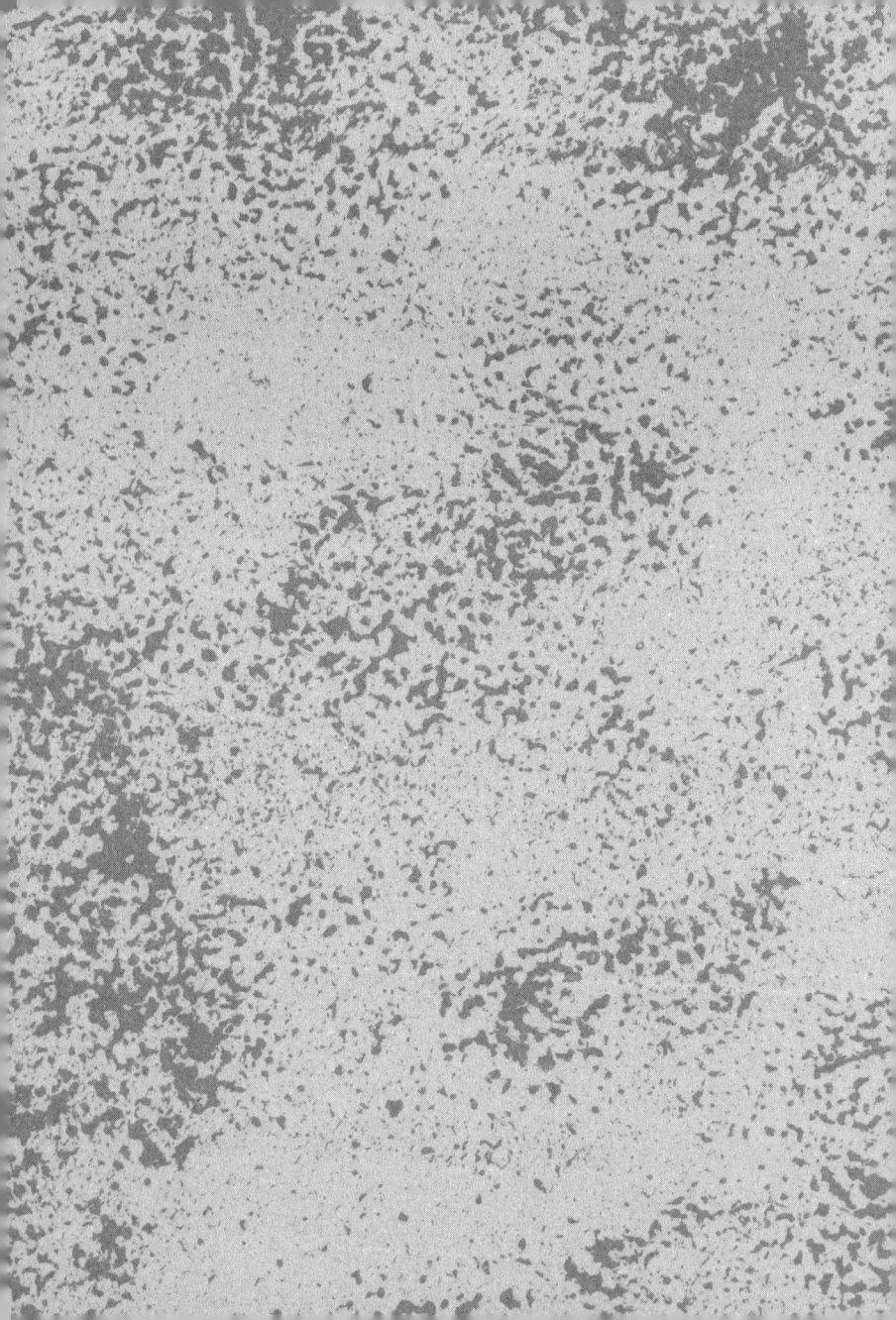

Today you bid farewell to the friendly security of this academic environment, a setting that will remain dear to you as long as the cords of memory shall lengthen.

And now you prepare to enter the
clamorous highways of life.

And as you go out today, I would
like to discuss with you some
aspects of the American dream.

For in a real sense,
America is essentially a dream,
a dream yet unfulfilled.

It is a dream of a land where men of all races, of all nationalities and all creeds can live together as brothers.

The substance of the dream is expressed in these sublime words, words lifted to cosmic proportions:

"We hold these truths to be self-evident, that all men are created equal, that they are endowed by their Creator with certain unalienable Rights, that among these are Life, Liberty and the pursuit of Happiness."

This is the dream.

Now one of the first things we notice in this dream is an amazing universal-ism.

It does not say some men,
but it says all men.

It does not say all white men, but it says all men, which includes Black men.

It does not say all Gentiles, but it says all men, which includes Jews.

It does not say all Protestants, but it says all men, which includes Catholics.

That is another thing we see in this dream that ultimately distinguishes democracy and our form of government with all of the totalitarian regimes that emerge in history.

It says that each individual has certain basic rights that are neither conferred by nor derived from the state.

In order to discover where they came from it is necessary to move back behind the dim mist of eternity, they are God-given.

And very seldom if ever in the history of the world has a sociopolitical document expressed in such profound, eloquent and unequivocal language the dignity and the worth of human personality.

The American dream reminds us that every man is the heir to the legacy of worthiness.

Ever since the Founding Fathers of our nation dreamed this noble dream, America has been something of a schizophrenic personality, tragically divided against herself.

On the one hand we have proudly professed the principles of democracy, and on the other hand we have sadly practiced the very antithesis of those principles.

Indeed slavery and segregation have been strange paradoxes in a nation founded on the principle that all men are created equal.

This is what the Swedish sociologist
Gunnar Myrdal referred to as
the American dilemma.

But now more than ever before,
America is challenged to bring
this noble dream into reality.

But the shape of the world today
does not permit us the luxury
of an anemic democracy.

And the price that America must pay for the continued exploitation of the Negro and other minority groups is the price of its own destruction.

The hour is late; the clock of destiny is ticking out.

It is trite, but urgently true, that
if America is to remain a
first-class nation she can no longer
have second-class citizens.

And so those individuals who are
working to implement the American
dream are the true saviors of democracy.

Now may I suggest some of the things we must do if we are to make the American dream a reality.

First I think all of us must develop a world perspective.

Certainly every member of this graduating class, and all of us assembled here this afternoon, must come to see that if we are to survive today, we must have a world perspective, for the American dream will not become a reality devoid of the larger dream of the world of brotherhood and peace and goodwill.

The world in which we live is a world of geographical oneness and we are challenged now to make it spiritually one.

Now it is true that the geographical togetherness of this generation has come into being to a large extent through man's scientific ingenuity.

Modern man through his scientific and technological genius has been able to dwarf distance and place time in chains.

Now jet planes have compressed into minutes distances that once took days and months.

I think Bob Hope has adequately described this jet age in which we live, and it is not at all the common thing for a preacher to be quoting Bob Hope, but I think he's described it so well that it's fitting to quote it, he says, "It is an age in which it is possible to take a nonstop flight from Los Angeles, California, to New York City, and if once taken off in Los Angeles you develop hiccups, you will hic in Los Angeles and cup in New York City."

That's really moving.

You know it is true because of the
time difference to take a flight from
Tokyo, Japan, on Sunday morning
and arrive in Seattle, Washington,
on the preceding Saturday night.

And when your friends meet you at the
airport and ask when you left Tokyo,
you will have to say I left tomorrow.

This is the kind of world
in which we live.

Now this is a bit humorous but I'm
trying to laugh a basic fact into all of
us, and it is simply this, that the world
in which we live is geographically one.

Through our scientific genius, we have
made of this world a neighborhood.

Now, through our moral and
spiritual development we must
make of it a brotherhood.

In a real sense, we must all learn
to live together as brothers.

Or we will all perish together as fools.

We must come to see that no individual can live alone; no nation can live alone.

We must all live together; we must all be concerned about each other.

Some months ago, Mrs. King and
I journeyed to that great country
in the Far East known as India.

I never will forget the experiences that
came to us as we moved around that
great country, or the opportunity of
talking and meeting with the great
leaders of India and talking and
meeting with people all over in the
cities and the villages throughout India.

Certainly this was an experience
that I will always remember, but I
submit to you this afternoon that there
were those depressing moments.

How can one avoid being depressed
when he sees with his own eyes
millions of people going to bed
hungered at night? How can one
avoid being depressed when he sees
with his own eyes millions of people
sleeping on the sidewalks at night?

In Calcutta alone, more than
a million people sleep on the
sidewalks every night.

In Bombay, more than six
hundred thousand people sleep
on the sidewalks every night.

They have no beds to sleep in;
they have no houses to go in.

How can one avoid being depressed when he discovers that out of India's population, 400 million people, more than 365 million make an annual income of less than 60 dollars a year?

Most of these people have never seen a doctor or a dentist.

As I looked at these conditions, I found myself saying, "Can we in America stand idly by and not be concerned?"

Then something within me cried out, "Oh, no, because the destiny of the United States is tied up with the destiny of India—with the destiny of every other nation."

And I thought about the fact that we spend more than a million dollars a day to store surplus food in this country.

I said to myself, "I know where we can store that food free of charge— in the wrinkled stomachs of the hundreds of millions of people who go to bed hungered at night."

Maybe we spend too much of
our national budget establishing
military bases around the world,
rather than bases of genuine
concern and understanding.

All I'm saying is simply this,
that all life is interrelated.

We are caught in an inescapable network of mutuality; tied in a single garment of destiny.

And so whatever affects one directly, affects all indirectly.

As long as there is poverty in this world, no man can be totally rich even if he has a billion dollars.

As long as diseases are rampant and
millions of people cannot expect to
live more than twenty or thirty years,
no man can be totally healthy, even
if he just got a clean bill of health
from the finest clinic of America.

Strangely enough, I can never
be what I ought to be until you
are what you ought to be.

You can never be what you ought to be until I am what I ought to be.

This is the way the world is made.

I didn't make it that way, but this is the interrelated structure of reality.

John Donne caught it a few years ago and could cry out, "No man is an island entire of itself; every man is a piece of the continent, a part of the main."

He goes on toward the end to say, "Any man's death diminishes me, because I am involved in mankind, and therefore never send to know for whom the bell tolls; it tolls for thee."

If we are to realize the American dream
we must cultivate this world perspective.

That is another thing
quite related to this.

We must keep our moral and spiritual
progress abreast with our scientific
and technological advances.

This is something of the
dilemma of modern man.

We have allowed our civilization
to outdistance our culture.

The problem is pointed out somewhat
by Professor MacIver following the
German sociologist Alfred Weber
in pointing out the distinction
between culture and civilization.

Civilization refers to what we use;
culture refers to what we are.

Civilization is that complex of devices,
instrumentalities, mechanisms and
techniques by means of which we live.

Culture is that realm of ends
expressed in art, literature, religion
and morals for which at best we live.

The great problem confronting us
today is that we have allowed the
means by which we live to outdistance
the ends for which we live.

The problem is we have allowed our
civilization to outrun our culture,
and so we are in danger now of
ending up with guided missiles in
the hands of misguided men.

This is what the poet Thoreau meant when he said, "Improved means to an unimproved end."

If we are to survive today and realize the dream of our mission and the dream of the world, we must bridge the gulf and somehow keep the means by which we live abreast with the ends for which we live.

Another thing that must be done is, we must get rid of the notion once and for all that there are superior and inferior races.

Now we know that this view still lags around in spite of the fact that many great anthropologists, such as Margaret Mead and Ruth Benedict and Melville Herskovits and others have pointed out and made it clear through scientific evidence that there are no superior races and there are no inferior races.

That there may be superior individuals
intellectually within all races.

That there are four types of blood
and that these types of blood
are found within all races.

But in spite of all this evidence, however, the view still gets around somehow that there are superior races and that there are inferior races.

The whole philosophy of white supremacy is based on this.

Now we do it this day in a different way than they used to do it.

You know, there was a time when some people used to argue the inferiority of the Negro and the colored races generally on the basis of the Bible and religion.

They could say the Negro was inferior by nature because of Noah's curse upon the children of Ham.

And then one brother had probably
read the logic of Aristotle.

You know Aristotle brought into
being the syllogism which had a
major premise and a minor premise
and a conclusion, and one brother
had probably read Aristotle and he
put his argument in the framework
of an Aristotelian syllogism.

He could say all men are made
in the image of God.

This was a major premise.

And then came his minor
premise: God, as everybody
knows, is not a Negro.

Therefore the Negro is not a man.

Now he had reasoned it out on the basis of his logical structure.

But you see today, we don't hear these arguments much.

It's set out on sociological
and cultural grounds.

"The Negro is not culturally ready for
integration, and if integration comes
into being it will pull the white race
back a generation. In order to work it
out, it will take fifty or seventy-five years
in order to pull up these standards."

And then we hear that the Negro is criminal, he's a criminal, and there are those who would almost say he is a criminal by nature.

Now they never point out that these things are environmental and not racial; and these problems are problems of urban dislocation.

And they never point out, or rather
they fail to see, that poverty, and
disease, and ignorance breed crime
whatever the racial group may be.

And it is a tortuous logic that views
the tragic results of segregation
and discrimination as an argument
for the continuation of it.

If we are to implement the American dream we must get rid of the notion once and for all that there are superior and inferior races.

This means that members of minority groups must make it clear that they can use their resources even though oppression is still there.

And so we must make full
and constructive use of the
freedom we already possess.

We must not use our oppression as an
excuse for mediocrity and laziness.

For history has proven that inner
determination can often break through
the outer shackles of circumstance.

Take the Jews, for example, and
the years they have been forced
to walk through the long and
desolate night of oppression.

This did not keep them
from rising up to plunge against
cloud-filled nights of oppression, new
and blazing stars of inspiration.

And so being a Jew did not keep
Handel from lifting his vision to
high heaven and emerging with the
inspiration to leave for unfolding
generations the glad thunders and
gentle signs of a great messiah.

Being a Jew did not keep Einstein
from using his genius-packed
mind to challenge an axiom,
and leave for the lofty sights of
science a theory of relativity.

And so, being a Negro does not have to keep any individual from rising up to make a contribution at this hour, and we already have numerous and inspiring examples of Negroes who have revealed in their own lives.

Human nature cannot be catalogued, and we need not wait until the day of full emancipation.

So from an old slave cabin in Virginia's
hills, Booker T. Washington rose up to
be one of the nation's greatest leaders.

He lit a torch in Alabama,
then darkness fled.

From the red hills of Gordon County,
Georgia, from an iron foundry at
Chattanooga, Tennessee, from the
arms of a mother who could neither
read nor write, Roland Hayes rose
up to be one of the nation's and
the world's greatest singers.

He carried his melodious voice to the mansion of the Queen Mother of Spain and the palace of King George V.

From the poverty-stricken areas of Philadelphia, Pennsylvania, Marian Anderson rose up to be the world's greatest contralto, so that Toscanini could say that a voice like this comes only once in a century.

Sibelius of Finland could say,
"My roof is too low for such a voice."

From humble, crippling circumstances,
George Washington Carver rose up
and carved for himself an imperishable
niche in the annals of science.

There was a star in the sky
of female leadership.

Then came Mary McLeod Bethune and
grabbed it and allowed it to shine in
her life, with all of its radiating beauty.

There was a star in the diplomatic sky.

Then came Ralph Bunche,

the grandson of a slave preacher,

and allowed it to shine in his life

with all of its radiant beauty.

There was a star in the athletic sky.

Then came Joe Louis with his educated fists, Jesse Owens with his fleet and dashing feet, Jackie Robinson with his powerful bat and calm spirit.

All of these people have come to remind us that we need not wait until the day of full emancipation.

They have justified the
conviction of the poet that:

Fleecy locks and Black complexion
Cannot forfeit nature's claim.
Skin may differ but affection
Dwells in black and white the same.
Were I so tall as to reach the pole
Or to grasp the ocean at a span,
I must be measured by my soul,
The mind is standard of the man.

Finally, if we are to implement the American dream, we must continue to engage in creative protest in order to break down all of those barriers that make it impossible for the dream to be realized.

Now I know there are those people who will argue that we must wait on something.

They fail to see the necessity for creative protest, but I say to you this afternoon that I can see no way to break loose from an old order and move into a new order without standing up, resisting the unjust systems of the old order.

In order to do this, we must get rid of two strange illusions that have been held by the so-called moderates in race relations.

First, that is the myth of time.

Those people who say that you must wait on time, and if you "just wait and be patient," time will work this situation out.

And so, they will say this even
about freedom rides.*

They will say this about sit-ins: that
you're pushing things too fast—cool
off—time will work these problems out.

---

* In May, 1961, the Congress of Racial Equality, an interracial direct-
action group founded in 1942, sent buses of "Freedom Riders" into the
South to test segregation laws and practices in interstate transportation. In Alabama and Mississippi the Freedom Riders were attacked
by white racist mobs and arrested, but on September 22, 1961, the Inter
state Commerce Commission ruled that passengers on interstate carriers would be seated without regard to race and that such carriers could
not use segregated terminals.

Well, evolution may be true in
the biological realm, and at that
point Darwin was right.

But when a Herbert Spencer seeks
to apply to the whole of society
"evolution," there is no truth in it.[*]

---

[*] Herbert Spencer (1820–1903) was the formulator of "social Darwin-ism," an effort to apply Darwinism to society; he stressed, among other points, that Anglo-Saxon civilization was a superior development out of previous civilizations and the result of competition.

Even a superficial look at history
reveals to us that social progress never
rolls in on the wheels of inevitability.

It comes through the tireless
efforts and the persistent work
of dedicated individuals.

Without this hard work, time itself
becomes an ally of the insurgent
and primitive forces of irrational
emotionalism and social stagnation.

And so we must get rid
of the myth of time.

That is another myth, which bases itself
on a sort of educational determinism.

And it is an argument that you can't solve this problem through legislation.

You can't solve this problem through judicial decrees.

You can't solve this problem through executive orders on the part of the president of the United States.

It must be solved by education.

Now I agree that education plays a great role, and it must continue to play a great role in changing attitudes, in getting people ready for the new order.

And we must also see the importance of legislation.

It is not either education or legislation.

It is both education and legislation.

Now, people will say,
"Well, you can't legislate morals."

Well, that may be true.

Even though morality may not be
legislated, behavior can be regulated.

And this is very important.

We need religion and education
to change attitudes and to
change the hearts of men.

We need legislation and federal action to control behavior.

It may be true that the law can't make a man love me, but it can keep him from lynching me, and I think that's pretty important also.

And so we must get rid of these illusions and move on with determination and with zeal to break down the unjust system we find in our society, so that it will be possible to realize the American dream.

As I have said so often, if we seek to break down the system, we must do it with the proper methods.

I am convinced more than ever before that, as the powerful, creative way opens, men and women who are willing to break the barriers of oppression and of segregation and discrimination, they need not fall down to the levels of violence.

They need not sink into the quicksands of hatred.

They can stand on the high
ground of noninjury, love and
soul force, and turn this nation
upside down and right side up.

I so believe, more than ever before,
in the power of nonviolent resistance.

It has a moral aspect tied to it.

It makes it possible for the individual to secure moral ends through moral means.

This has been one of the great debates through history.

People have felt that it is impossible to achieve moral ends through moral means.

And so a Machiavelli could come into being and set forth a sort of duality within the moral structure of the universe.

Even communism could come into being and say that anything justifies the end of a classless society—lying, deceit, hate, violence, anything.

And this is where nonviolent resistance breaks with communism and all of those theories that would argue that the end justifies the means, because we realize that the end is preexistent in the means.

In the long run of history, destructive means cannot bring about constructive ends.

That is a practical aspect
about this method.

It exposes the moral defenses
of the opponent.

Not only that, it somehow arouses
his conscience at the same time,
and it breaks down his morale.

He has no answer for it.

If he puts you in jail, that's all right.

If he lets you out, that's all right.

If he beats you, you accept that.

If he doesn't beat you—fine.

And so you go on, leaving

him with no answer.

But if you use violence,

he does have an answer.

He has the whole machinery

of the state.

He has the state militia.

He has police brutality.

But now he doesn't have an answer.

And that is the power in it.

And it is one of the most magnificent
expressions going on today.

For we see it in the movement taking place on the part of students in the South and their allies who have been willing to come in from the North and other sections.

They have taken our deep groans and passionate yearnings, filtered them in their own souls, and fashioned them into the creative protest, which is an epic known all over our nation.

They have moved in a uniquely meaningful orbit, imparting light and heat to a distant satellite.

And people say, "Does this bring results?" Well, look at it.

In less than a year, more than 142 cities of the Deep South have integrated their lunch counters, and this was done without a single court suit.

It was done without spending millions and millions of dollars.

We think of the freedom rides,
and think of the fact that more
than sixty-five people are now in
jail in Jackson, Mississippi.

"What has this done?" we say.

These people have been beaten.

They have suffered.

Let us realize that brought to the attention of this nation, the indignities and injustices Negro people still confront in interstate travel.

So, it has had an educational value.

But not only that—signs have come down from bus stations in Montgomery, Alabama.

They've never been down before.

Not only that—the attorney general
of this nation has called on ICC
to come out with new regulations
making it powerfully clear that
segregation in interstate travel is
illegal and unconstitutional.

And so this method can bring results.

Sometimes it can bring quick results.

But even when it doesn't bring
immediate results, it is at all times
working on the conscience.

It is at all times adhering
to moral means in order to
bring about moral ends.

And so I say that we must continue on the way of creative protest.

And I believe also that this method will help us in going into the new age with the proper attitude.

As I have said in so many instances, it is not enough to struggle for the new society.

We must make sure that we make
the psychological adjustment
to live in that new society.

This is true of white people, and
it is true of Negro people.

And so it will save white people
from going into the new age
with old vestiges of prejudice and
attitudes of white supremacy.

It will save the Negro from going in
to substitute one tyranny for another.

And I know sometimes
we get discouraged and
sometimes disappointed with
the slow pace of things.

And so at times we begin to talk about racial separation instead of racial integration, feeling that there is no other way out.

I can only say to that that the problem never will be solved by substituting one tyranny for another.

Black supremacy is as dangerous as white supremacy, and God is not interested merely in the freedom of Black men and brown men and yellow men.

God is interested in the freedom of the whole human race and in the creation of a society where all men can live together as brothers, and every man will respect the dignity and the worth of human personality.

And not only this, by following this method, we may be able to teach our world something that it so desperately needs at this hour.

In a day when Sputniks and Freedom 7s are dashing through outer space, and guided ballistic missiles are carving highways of death through the stratosphere, no nation can win a war.

The choice is no longer a choice between violence and nonviolence.

It is either nonviolence or nonexistence.

Unless we find some alternative to war, we will destroy ourselves by the misuse of our own instruments.

And so, with all of these attitudes and principles working together, I believe we will be able to make a contribution as men of good will to the ongoing structure of our society toward the realization of the American dream.

And so, as you go out today, I call upon you not to be detached spectators, but involved participants, in this great drama that is taking place in our nation and around the world.

You know, there are certain words in every academic discipline that become a part of the technical vocabulary of that discipline after a period of time.

Every academic discipline has its technical nomenclature, and modern psychology has a word that is used, probably, more than any other word in modern psychology.

It is the word maladjusted.

This word is the ringing cry of modern
child psychology. *Maladjusted*.

Certainly all of us want to live
a well-adjusted life in order to
avoid the neurotic personality.

But I say to you, this evening, there are certain things within our social order to which I am proud to be maladjusted and to which I call upon all men of good will to be maladjusted.

So, if you will allow the preacher in me to come out now, let me say to you that I never did intend to adjust to the evils of segregation and discrimination. I never did intend to adjust myself to religious bigotry.

I never did intend to adjust myself to economic conditions that will take necessities from the many to give luxuries to the few.

I never did intend to adjust myself to the madness of militarism, and the self-defeating effects of physical violence.

And I call upon all men of good will to be maladjusted because it may well be that the salvation of our world lies in the hands of the maladjusted.

And so let us be maladjusted, as maladjusted as the prophet Amos, who in the midst of the injustices of his day could cry out in words that echo across the centuries, "Let justice run down like waters and righteousness like a mighty stream."

Let us be as maladjusted as Abraham Lincoln, who had the vision to see that this nation could not exist half slave and half free.

Let us be maladjusted as Jesus of Nazareth, who could look into the eyes of the men and women of his generation and cry out, "Love your enemies. Bless them that curse you. Pray for them that despitefully use you."

And I believe that it is through such maladjustment that we will be able to emerge from the bleak and desolate midnight of man's inhumanity to man into the bright and glittering daybreak of freedom and justice.

And this will be the day when all of God's children, Black men and white men, Jews and Gentiles, Catholics and Protestants, will be able to join hands and sing in the words of the old Negro spiritual, "Free at last! Free at last! Thank God almighty, we are free at last!"

About Dr. Martin Luther King Jr.

Dr. Martin Luther King Jr. (1929–1968), preacher, civil rights leader, and recipient of the Nobel Peace Prize, inspired and sustained the struggle for freedom, interracial brotherhood, and social justice through his philosophy and strategies of nonviolence.

About Yolanda Renee King

Yolanda Renee King is the daughter of Martin Luther King III and Arndrea Waters King. She is the only grandchild of Dr. Martin Luther King Jr. and Mrs. Coretta Scott King.